Windsor

ETON, ASCOT AND RUNNYMEDE

W indsor Castle is probably the largest fortress of its kind in the world, and has belonged continuously to the sovereigns of England for over 900 years. It is still the setting for great ceremonies of state, and houses many of the priceless treasures in the Royal Collection.

The Castle began as a simple timber stockade on a mound, one of a ring of strongholds built around London by William the Conqueror soon after 1066 to keep the hostile population at bay. It took its name from a small hunting-lodge nearby, in the Saxon settlement of Windlesora.

Over the years Windsor became more and more important as a royal residence. Edward III's reign saw the foundation of the Order of the Garter, the most prestigious Order of the realm, with a colourful ceremony which annually brings pomp and pageantry to the town. Edward IV began the splendid Gothic chapel of St George, and Charles II and George IV were both to leave their regal stamp on Windsor. But the ultimate accolade came in 1917 when George V declared that henceforth his family and descendants would take the surname Windsor. Windsor and the Royal Family were thus indissolubly linked, and rightly so, for though it is much else besides, Windsor is indeed the royal home of kings.

The Castle Precincts are divided into three main areas – the Lower, Middle and Upper Wards. The Lower Ward is entered through the King Henry VIII Gate, and opposite this is St George's Chapel. To the left of the Chapel a smaller gateway leads to Horseshoe Cloister, an attractive row of brick and timbered houses dating from the 15th century. Past St George's Chapel is the Albert Memorial Chapel, converted by Queen Victoria in remembrance of her beloved husband who died in 1861.

The Middle Ward is dominated by the Round Tower, built by King Henry II in the 12th century on the mound raised by William the Conqueror. This was the Castle's main stronghold, its strategic importance lying in the views stretching for miles across the Thames Valley.

Within the Upper Ward are the State Apartments, a magnificent suite of ceremonial rooms

RIGHT: *An aerial view of Windsor Castle. The medieval Round Tower dominates the Castle Precincts and surrounding area.*

ABOVE: *The bronze statue of Queen Victoria was erected to commemorate* *the Queen's Golden Jubilee in 1887.*

containing important paintings, tapestries and furniture, and the Private Apartments of Her Majesty The Queen. The Royal Standard is flown when The Queen is in residence.

A daily guard is mounted at Windsor Castle, usually provided by one of the regiments of Foot Guards.

BELOW: *The band of the Coldstream Guards plays at the Changing of the Guard.*

The State Apartments

LEFT: *A magnificent suit of armour made for Henry VIII in 1540.*

RIGHT: *The Grand Staircase, designed in 1866, is dominated by a statue of George IV.*

BELOW: *The Waterloo Chamber, used as a banqueting room, contains portraits of those who took part in the defeat of Napoleon in 1815.*

OPPOSITE LEFT: *Paintings by Canaletto decorate the walls of the King's State Bedchamber. Purple and green hangings were placed on the bed for the State Visit of Napoleon III and Empress Eugénie in 1815.*

RIGHT: *The Queen's Presence Chamber has a fine painted ceiling by Verrio, tapestries from the French Gobelins factory, a fireplace by Robert Adam and exquisite wood carving by Grinling Gibbons.*

BELOW LEFT: *Militaria is on display in the Queen's Guard Chamber.*

BELOW RIGHT: *The Queen's Drawing Room was originally a sitting room for Catherine of Braganza, wife of Charles II.*

St George's Chapel

One of the most beautiful religious buildings in England, St George's Chapel was begun in 1475 by King Edward IV as the chapel of the Order of the Garter. The Order, which was founded in 1348 by Edward III, is Britain's highest order of chivalry and is said to have its origin in a delightful story. Tradition has it that at a ball held to celebrate the capture of Calais in 1387 a lady's garter fell to the ground. The King picked it up and, seeing his courtiers smile, said, 'Honi soit qui mal y pense' – 'Shame on him who thinks evil of it'.

There are 24 Knights of the Garter who walk in procession through the Castle Precincts to attend an annual service with the Sovereign of the Order. Their stall plates and colourful banners can be seen in the choir.

Built in the Perpendicular style of Gothic architecture, the chapel took 51 years to complete. Ten monarchs are buried here, including Edward IV himself, Henry VI and Henry VIII.

ABOVE: *The Queen and Duke of Edinburgh in full Garter robes and insignia.*

RIGHT: *The banners of the Knights of the Garter hang in the choir of St George's Chapel, which dates from 1475.*

LEFT: *The Queen, The Queen Mother and The Prince of Wales leave St George's Chapel after the annual Garter service.*

BELOW: *The High Altar of St George's Chapel.*

Queen Mary's Dolls' House

LEFT: *Queen Mary's Dolls' House, built in 1921–4, was fitted with electric lighting. The scale of the house is one-twelfth of actual size.*

BELOW: *An embroideress spent 1,500 hours sewing the minute Royal monograms on the tiny items of linen.*

Queen Mary's Dolls' House is a delightful miniature residence. Perfect in every tiny detail, it was designed by Sir Edwin Lutyens in 1921–4 for the wife of King George V. Completely up to date at the time it was built, its furniture, fittings, utensils and gadgets were supplied to scale by well-known manufacturers. Many fine craftsmen and artists were involved in the exquisite workmanship of its contents and decoration. They have provided an accurate and endlessly fascinating record of the priceless treasures and daily paraphernalia of a great house in the early 20th century.

RIGHT: *The King's Bathroom is luxuriously finished in green and white marble. The silver taps are fully operational and supply running water.*

ABOVE: *Silk damask covers the walls of the Queen's Bedroom. The quilt is embroidered with seed pearls, and the carpet is of exquisite tapestry work in the style of Aubusson.*

LEFT: *The Dining Room is furnished with carved walnut chairs and side-tables. On the dining table are set silverware, glasses and porcelain fruit dishes.*

This vast park, which extends over an area of about 4,800 acres, is the remains of a former royal hunting forest. Today much of it is open to the public, and red deer now graze peacefully, reintroduced by The Queen in celebration of her Silver Jubilee in 1977.

From the Castle grounds the magnificent Long Walk stretches for three miles to the Copper Horse statue of George III. Other interesting edifices within the park include The Ruins, fragments of Roman buildings brought from Libya in 1817, The Indian Kiosk and a totem pole erected to mark the centenary of British Columbia, Canada.

Notable planted areas are the Woodland Garden, the Savill Garden and the Valley Gardens, which feature superb displays of herbaceous plants, azaleas, rhododendrons and heathers.

At the southern edge of the park is Virginia Water (said to have been named after Elizabeth I, the Virgin Queen). The lake, which is almost two miles long, was created under the direction of William, Duke of Cumberland, by his troops who had fought at the Battle of Culloden in 1746. The duke's exploits are commemorated by an obelisk erected by his father, George II.

RIGHT: *Red deer were reintroduced into the park from Balmoral to celebrate The Queen's Silver Jubilee in 1977.*

BELOW: *The Long Walk leads through Windsor Great Park to the King George IV Gate, the entrance used by State Visitors to Windsor Castle.*

LEFT: *The Ruins, fragments of Roman buildings brought from Libya in 1817.*

CENTRE LEFT: *The Copper Horse statue of George III.*

BELOW: *The colourful totem pole which marks the centenary of British Columbia, Canada.*

RIGHT: *Virginia Water, originally created from a stream in 1746, was enlarged and redesigned after a flood in 1768.*

Frogmore House, bought by Queen Charlotte in 1792, was enlarged in the classical style by the architect James Wyatt. Queen Charlotte is also responsible for the landscaping of its magnificent setting.

Frogmore Garden was much loved and enjoyed by Queen Victoria and her husband Prince Albert. It is in this delightful setting that the Queen's mother, Victoria Duchess of Kent, was buried and here, too, in the Royal Mausoleum, that the royal couple themselves chose to be interred. The Royal Mausoleum and the garden at Frogmore are open to the public on two days each May by gracious permission of Her Majesty The Queen. Other members of the Royal Family are buried in a small cemetery nearby.

Various shows take place annually in Windsor Great Park, notably the Royal Windsor Horse Show in the Home Park Public. This event featuring equestrian competition and displays is held over five days. The Queen also graciously opens the Home Park Private to the public for the Royal Windsor Rose Show each midsummer.

Among regular leisure activities taking place in the park during the summer season is polo on Smith's Lawn.

BELOW: *Queen Victoria and Prince Albert are buried in the Royal Mausoleum.*

RIGHT: *Frogmore House was bought by Queen Charlotte in 1792.*

ABOVE RIGHT: *Caractacus, the stately drum horse of The Blues and Royals, at the Royal Windsor Horse Show.*

LEFT: *Prince Charles playing polo on Smith's Lawn.*

RIGHT: *Queen Victoria's Teahouse in Frogmore Garden.*

Map of Windsor

RIGHT: *Map of modern Windsor.*

BELOW: *John Norden's map of Windsor drawn in 1607. The Castle Precincts are clearly shown, as is the Parish Church and the area surrounding Church Street. Behind the Elizabethan market hall, built on stilts, is a pillory. Of the two inns shown with their signs opposite the Castle, one was immortalized by Shakespeare as* The Garter Inn *in* The Merry Wives of Windsor.

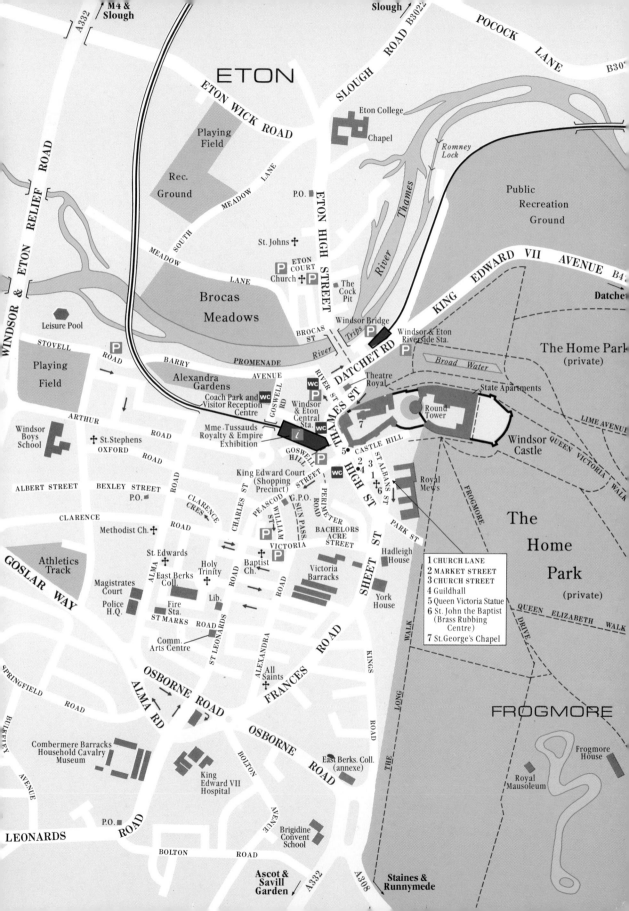

The town of Windsor grew up around the Castle in the Middle Ages and many of its buildings have interesting historical links. Within the cobbled area is the quaint Market Cross House, which commemorates the market cross removed in the 17th century. Church Street features a number of fine houses, among them one said to have been lived in by Nell Gwynn.

The Guildhall was begun in 1687 and completed by Sir Christopher Wren, whose father was Dean of Windsor. The story goes that the townspeople were concerned that the slender outer pillars were not strong enough to support the upper chamber and asked Wren to add pillars in the centre. He did so, but in fact made them a little shorter than the others to prove that his original design was sound.

The Parish Church of St John the Baptist was founded in 1110, but the present church was built in the early 19th century. In the registers of the old church is recorded the burial in St George's Chapel of Charles I after his execution.

RIGHT: *Elegant 18th-century houses in Park Street.*

BELOW: *The Guildhall, completed by Sir Christopher Wren. The statue on the south front is of Prince George of Denmark, consort of Queen Anne.*

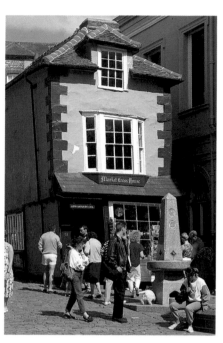

LEFT: *Market Cross House.*

BELOW LEFT: *Among the many historic buildings in the cobbled area of Church Street is a house in which Nell Gwynn is said to have lived.*

RIGHT: *The Parish Church of St John the Baptist.*

CENTRE RIGHT: *A 15th-century building in Church Lane.*

BOTTOM RIGHT: *Western Cottage, Bachelor's Acre, where the Reverend S. J. Stone wrote the hymn 'The Church's one foundation'.*

ABOVE: *Full dress coat and waistcoat of an officer of The Blues, 1795–1812, on display at The Household Cavalry Museum. An identical coat was worn by George III when he was a Captain in The Blues.*

ABOVE: *The Queen's Presents and Royal Carriages are on display at the Royal Mews. This is a semi-state landau.*

LEFT: *The Royalty and Empire Exhibition recreates the celebrations for Queen Victoria's Diamond Jubilee in 1897.*

RIGHT: *Queen Victoria's charabanc can be seen at the Royal Mews.*

O n a sunny day in summer, one of
Windsor's great attractions is the River
Thames, always lively with boats of
all kinds, while the swans glide lazily
up and down. Brightly painted narrow-boats are
often moored alongside the motor launches of
holidaymakers. Rowing boats or motor boats can
be hired and there is a choice of pleasure-boat
trips. For serious rowers the Thames provides a
challenging and enjoyable course.

'Sweet Themmes runne softly, till I end my Song.'
EDMUND SPENSER

ABOVE: *Etonians*
celebrate the Fourth of
June, George III's
birthday, with a
procession of boats.

ABOVE RIGHT: *Visitors to*
the area can hire a
rowing boat or take a
pleasure-boat trip on the
River Thames.

RIGHT: *Rafts, one of*
Eton's boathouses, with
Windsor Bridge in the
background.

ABOVE: *An autumnal afternoon's boating in the shelter of Windsor Castle.*

LEFT: *Eton College, the most famous school in the world, situated on the River Thames. This is the view described by Thomas Gray in his famous* Ode on a Distant Prospect of Eton College.

Just over Windsor Bridge is Eton, a historic town and home of the most famous school in the world. The High Street is lined with attractive old buildings and interesting antique shops. About halfway along is the Cock Pit, now a restaurant. In the 17th and 18th centuries cockfighting went on here, and Charles II is said to have frequented it. A pair of stocks is preserved outside, and on the corner is a rare Victorian pillar box.

RIGHT: An Etonian wearing the School Dress of black tailcoat and waistcoat with pin-striped trousers.

Eton College was founded in 1440 by King Henry VI, whose statue can be seen in School Yard. The College was intended to provide schooling and accommodation for 70 poor scholars. It was in the 17th century that it became a fashionable school for the sons of the nobility. Today there are about 1,200 fee-paying pupils, or 'oppidans', as well as the 70 scholars originally provided for. Boys wear distinctive traditional uniform of pin-stripes, tailcoats and wing collars. The long list of famous men who have been educated

BELOW: The Cock Pit in Eton High Street, said to have been frequented by Charles II. A pair of stocks stands outside, and on the corner is a Victorian pillar box.

at this school includes 20 prime ministers.

The college buildings, around the central quadrangle known as School Yard, include Lower School (1443), one of the oldest schoolrooms in the country still in use; Upper School, built in the 17th century; the 15th-century chapel, a magnificent example of Perpendicular Gothic architecture; and Lupton's Range, built in 1517. The passage under Lupton's Tower leads to the Cloisters and to the famous playing fields beyond.

ABOVE: *Eton College was founded in 1440 by Henry VI. His statue, which stands in School Yard, shows the* *Sovereign in Garter robes. In the background is Lupton's Tower.*

Royal Ascot is one of the traditional events of the British social and sporting calendar. A race meeting at Ascot was inaugurated by Queen Anne in 1711. Since then it has received varying degrees of royal and popular patronage. Today, however, its popularity is assured, partly because of the close interest The Queen herself takes in horse racing and the attendance of the Royal Family.

Royal Ascot is held in June and its garden-party atmosphere is enjoyed by all racegoers. Appearance is paramount. Many gentlemen sport top hat and tails, while ladies compete with each other to display the season's brightest and most outrageous fashions. An imaginative hat is regarded as an essential fashion accesssory for ladies.

BELOW: *The Queen and the Duke of Edinburgh arrive at Royal Ascot by carriage.*

LEFT: *The Prince and Princess of Wales amidst the bustle of smartly attired racegoers.*

RIGHT: *The sport of kings . . .*

LEFT: *The Royal Procession of carriages is a feature of the race meeting at Royal Ascot. Here The Queen Mother, a keen racegoer, is accompanied by Princess Anne.*

Three miles south-east of Windsor is Runnymede, famous as the place where King John signed the Magna Carta in 1215. The charter affirmed the individual's right to justice and liberty, and has always been regarded by Englishmen as their chief constitutional safeguard against unjust and arbitrary rule. It has also found a place in the American Constitution and influenced modern human rights charters.

On the wooded hillside overlooking the lush and peaceful meadow and the winding river stand two memorials – the Magna Carta Memorial (1957), given by the American Bar Association, and the John F. Kennedy Memorial, erected in 1965 on an acre of ground given to the USA in memory of the assassinated president.

High on the hill above is the Commonwealth Air Forces Memorial, a moving tribute to 'the men and women of the Air Forces of the British Commonwealth and Empire who lost their lives serving from bases in the United Kingdom and North-West Europe in the Second World War and who have no known grave'. A total of 20,455 names are recorded on stone panels around the colonnaded courtyard. The memorial was designed by Sir Edward Maufe and opened by The Queen in 1953. It stands in beautifully tended grounds and from its windows there is a breathtaking view across the Thames.

BELOW: The seal of King John placed on the original document submitted to him at Runnymede.

ABOVE: The view looking north from the Commonwealth Air Forces Memorial above Runnymede.

RIGHT: The Commonwealth Air Forces Memorial commemorates over 20,000 men and women of the Air Forces who lost their lives in the Second World War and who have no known grave.

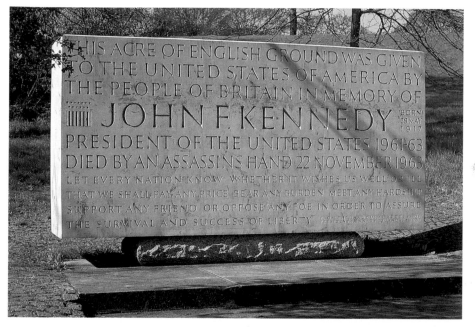

THIS ACRE OF ENGLISH GROUND WAS GIVEN TO THE UNITED STATES OF AMERICA BY THE PEOPLE OF BRITAIN IN MEMORY OF

JOHN F. KENNEDY BORN 29 MAY 1917

PRESIDENT OF THE UNITED STATES 1961-63 DIED BY AN ASSASSIN'S HAND 22 NOVEMBER 1963

LET EVERY NATION KNOW WHETHER IT WISHES US WELL OR ILL THAT WE SHALL PAY ANY PRICE BEAR ANY BURDEN MEET ANY HARDSHIP SUPPORT ANY FRIEND OR OPPOSE ANY FOE IN ORDER TO ASSURE THE SURVIVAL AND SUCCESS OF LIBERTY

LEFT: *The John F. Kennedy Memorial stands on an acre of land given to the USA in memory of the assassinated president.*

BELOW: *The Magna Carta Memorial was erected by the American Bar Association in 1957. It stands as a tribute to the freedom under law that was granted by Magna Carta.*

Windsor Safari Park

Set in 150 acres of parkland, Windsor Safari Park has proved to be a popular place to visit since it was first opened in 1970. The Park is built around an African theme and wild animals, including lions, tigers, elephants, giraffes, zebras and baboons, roam free in drive-through reserves.

Tropical World features tropical plants, butterflies and alligators. Other attractions include an African village, riverboat ride, a Sea World show with a killer whale, dolphins and sealions, a parrot show, chimpanzee enclosure, children's adventure playground and many other attractions and rides.

ABOVE: *Giraffes roam on the Serengeti Plain at Windsor Safari Park.*

ABOVE RIGHT: *Visitors to the Safari Park, built around an African theme, experience a different world as they take a boat trip along the Congo River.*

RIGHT: *Many of the animals at the Park are African, but it is also home to species from other continents, including tigers.*